Peru

Denise Allard

RSVP
RAINTREE
STECK-VAUGHN
P U B L I S H E R S
The Steck-Vaughn Company

Austin, Texas

Published by Raintree Steck-Vaughn Publishers, an imprint of Steck-Vaughn Company

A ZOË BOOK

Editors: Kath Davies, Pam Wells
Design: Sterling Associates
Map: Julian Baker
Production: Grahame Griffiths

Library of Congress Cataloging-in-Publication Data

Allard, Denise, 1952-.
    Peru / Denise Allard.
        p. cm. — (Postcards from)
    Includes index
    Summary: Brief descriptions of different places in Peru written in the form of postcards.
    ISBN 0-8172-4028-4. — ISBN 0-8172-6211-3 (pbk.)
    1. Peru—Description and travel—Juvenile literature. 2. Postcards—Peru—Juvenile literature. [1. Peru. 2. Postcards.] I. Title. II. Series.
F3425. A44 1997
985—dc20
                                                                96–1451
                                                                CIP
                                                                AC

Printed and bound in the United States
1 2 3 4 5 6 7 8 9 0 WZ 99 98 97 96

Photographic acknowledgments

The publishers wish to acknowledge, with thanks, the following photographic sources:

The Hutchison Library / Jeremy A.Horner 6; Impact Photos / Colin Jones 18, 20; / Michael Mirecki 24; South American Pictures / Tony Morrison - cover, title page, 8, 10, 12, 14, 16, 22, 26, 28.

The publishers have made every effort to trace the copyright holders, but if they have inadvertently overlooked any, they will be pleased to make the necessary arrangement at the first opportunity.

Contents

All the words that appear in **bold** are explained in the Glossary on page 30.

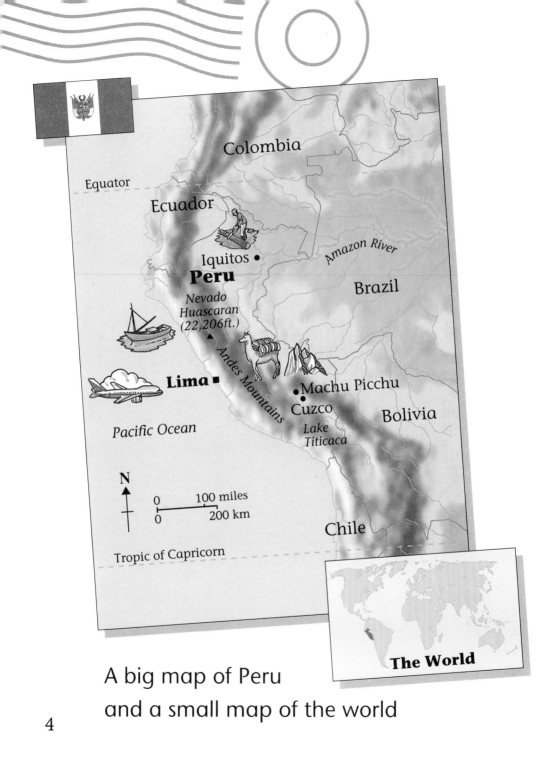

Colombia

Equator

Ecuador

Iquitos •

Peru

Nevado
Huascaran
(22,206ft.)

Amazon River

Brazil

Machu Picchu

Lima ■

Cuzco

Bolivia

*Lake
Titicaca*

Pacific Ocean

Andes Mountains

N

0   100 miles

0   200 km

Chile

Tropic of Capricorn

The World

A big map of Peru
and a small map of the world

Dear Amy,

We are in South America. This country is called Peru. The plane took more than five hours to fly here from Miami. You can see Peru in red on the small map.

Love,

Eric

P.S. Mom says that the United States is about eight times bigger than Peru. More than 22 million people live in Peru. Most people here live beside the ocean.

The busy main square in Lima

Dear Nelson,

Lima is the **capital** city of Peru. About 500 years ago, people from Spain came to Peru. They ruled Peru for more than 200 years. That is why many buildings in Lima look Spanish.

Love,

Pam

P.S. Most people in Peru speak and write in Spanish. We are lucky that Mom can speak Spanish. She understands what the people here are saying.

Buying food at the market

Dear Paula,

People in Peru shop for food at the outdoor markets. I bought a good snack from a street stand. It was called *papa rellena*. It was a potato stuffed with vegetables and then fried.

Love,

Ella

P.S. Mom says that the Incas were one of the first peoples to live in Peru. People in Peru enjoy food that is cooked in the **traditional** Inca way.

A ferryboat on Lake Titicaca

Dear Ted,

This is the biggest lake in South America. It is called Lake Titicaca. It is high up in the mountains. The weather is cooler here. Many people live beside the lake.

Your friend,

William

P.S. We went for a ride across the lake on a **ferryboat**. It was full of people. From the boat, we saw a fisherman. He was in a boat that was made from **reeds** called *tortora*.

A railroad station in the Andes Mountains

Dear Clare,

Yesterday we rode on a train. It carried us across the Andes Mountains. The train was full of **tourists**. At the top of the mountains, Dad took some photos. The view was fantastic.

Love,

Liam

P.S. Dad says that most people in Peru travel by bus. In the high mountains, people ride on animals called llamas. Some places are so far out that you have to get there by plane.

Shopping in the mountains

Dear Hugo,

There are many villages high in the mountains. In one village, we bought some wool rugs. We paid for them with Peruvian money that is called *nuevo sol*.

See you soon,

James

P.S. Mom says that 700 years ago, the Incas ruled Peru. They ruled for about 200 years. The Incas were good farmers, builders, and craftspeople.

The ruins of Machu Picchu

Dear Petra,

We have reached the ruins of Machu Picchu. There are lots of tourists here. The Inca people built this ancient city. Nobody has lived in Machu Picchu for hundreds of years.

Your friend,

Rachel

P.S. Dad says that when the Spanish people came to Peru, they did not find Machu Picchu. The city stayed hidden for about 400 years. An explorer discovered it in 1911.

Houses on the Amazon River at Iquitos

Dear Jordan,

We are in the city of Iquitos. These floating houses are on the edge of the city. People travel by boat along the Amazon River to visit other towns and villages.

Love,

Elroy

P.S. The plane flew over mountains and **rain forests** to reach Iquitos. Iquitos is on an island in the Amazon River. It is very hot here in the **tropics**.

In the Amazon rain forest

Dear Ali,

The Amazon rain forest is full of plants, wild animals, and birds. In the forest, **native** peoples live by hunting for food. The people have lived this way for thousands of years.

Love,

Githa

P.S. Mom says the Amazon River begins in the Andes Mountains. It is the longest river in the world. Big ships can sail for about 3,000 miles along this river.

A fishing boat made from reeds

Dear Abigail,

Here we are beside the Pacific Ocean. The fishermen here use their long, narrow *tortora* reed boats. The people of Peru have used reed boats for hundreds of years.

Love,

Rose

P.S. We are staying in a brand new house near the beach. Mom says that not long ago, this place was a quiet fishing village. Now it is full of people on vacation.

Playing music on the street

Dear Jack,

I love the music in Peru. Everywhere you go there are *Mestizo* bands. Long ago, the Incas played music on the same kinds of instruments.

Love,

Megan

P.S. People in Peru like to enjoy themselves. They love soccer, basketball, and baseball. Today there was a **bullfight**. Many people think that bullfighting is cruel.

A big procession at a festival

Dear Sara,

Most people in Peru follow the **Christian** religion. People dress up for **festivals**. This one is called *Corpus Christi*. People walk together through the streets in a procession.

Love,

Tom

P.S. Dad says that there are many festivals in Peru. Some are part of the Christian religion. Others are to remember events from the time of the people called the Incas.

The flag of Peru at the
Government Palace, Lima

Dear Anna,

This has been the flag of Peru for more than 100 years. It has two red stripes and one white stripe. In the middle of the white stripe, there is a symbol. This stands for Peru.

Your friend,

Josh

P.S. Mom says that Peru is no longer ruled by Spain. The people of Peru choose their own leaders. This way of ruling is called a **democracy**.

Glossary

Bullfight: A fight between a man and a bull

Capital: The town or city where people who rule the country meet

Christians: People who follow the teachings of Jesus. Jesus lived about 2,000 years ago.

Democracy: A country where all the people choose the leaders they want to run the country

Ferryboat: A large boat that carries people across water

Festival: A time when people remember something or someone special from the past. People often sing and dance during a festival.

Native: Someone who was born in the place or part of the country where they live

P.S.: This stands for Post Script. A postscript is the part of a card or letter that is added at the end, after the person has signed it.

Rain forest: Forests near the middle of the Earth. The weather there is hot and wet.

Reeds: Plants that grow beside rivers or lakes. They have long, thin leaves that are very strong.

Tourist: A person who is on vacation away from home

Traditional: Something that has been done in the same way for a long time

Tropics: The lands that are near the middle of the Earth. The heat from the sun is strongest here. We draw lines on maps to show the position of the tropics.

Index